COOL CARS

MERCEDES-AMG GT

BY KAITLYN DULING

EPIC

BELLWETHER MEDIA ››› MINNEAPOLIS, MN

EPIC BOOKS are no ordinary books. They burst with intense action, high-speed heroics, and shadows of the unknown. Are you ready for an Epic adventure?

This edition first published in 2024 by Bellwether Media, Inc.

No part of this publication may be reproduced in whole or in part without written permission of the publisher. For information regarding permission, write to Bellwether Media, Inc., Attention: Permissions Department, 6012 Blue Circle Drive, Minnetonka, MN 55343.

Library of Congress Cataloging-in-Publication Data

LC record for Mercedes-AMG GT available at: https://lccn.loc.gov/2023036153

Text copyright © 2024 by Bellwether Media, Inc. EPIC and associated logos are trademarks and/or registered trademarks of Bellwether Media, Inc.

Editor: Rachael Barnes   Designer: Jeffrey Kollock

Printed in the United States of America, North Mankato, MN.

TABLE OF CONTENTS

TRAVELING IN STYLE	4
ALL ABOUT THE GT	6
PARTS OF THE GT	12
THE GT'S FUTURE	20
GLOSSARY	22
TO LEARN MORE	23
INDEX	24

TRAVELING IN STYLE »

A driver packs the trunk of their Mercedes-AMG GT. Now the **coupe** is ready for a road trip.

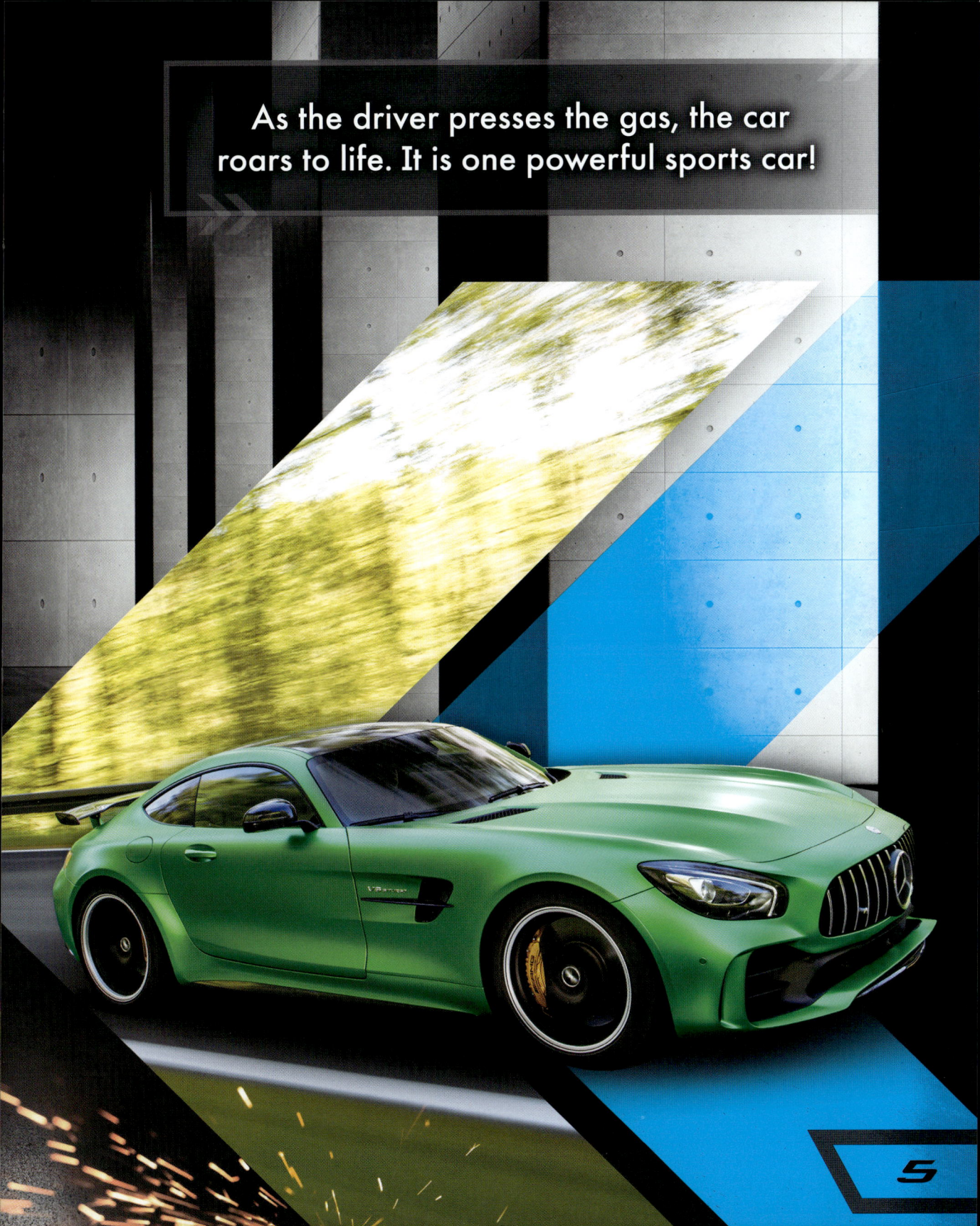
As the driver presses the gas, the car roars to life. It is one powerful sports car!

ALL ABOUT THE GT »

KARL BENZ

EARLY BENZ CARS

In 1883, Karl Benz started a company that made engines. Two years later, he built the world's first gas-powered car.

The company grew. In 2022, it became the Mercedes-Benz Group AG. It is based in Germany.

MERCEDES-BENZ GROUP AG OFFICES IN STUTTGART, GERMANY

WHERE IS IT MADE?

EUROPE

STUTTGART, GERMANY

Mercedes-Benz has made many different cars. The 300 SL and G-Class are famous **models**. AMG is part of Mercedes-Benz. It is known for making high-performing, **luxury** cars.

MERCEDES-AMG G 63

GT BASICS

YEAR FIRST MADE — 2014

COST — starting around $135,000

HOW MANY MADE — more than 17,000

FEATURES

- V8 engine
- front grille
- long hood

The GT was first released in 2014. *GT* stands for "grand tourer."

AMG GT RELEASE IN 2014

RACE READY

The GT helps out on the track. It is used as a safety car during famous car races.

SAFETY CAR

Like other GTs, the AMG GT is made for speed and comfort over long distances.

PARTS OF THE GT »

The GT's **V8 engine** sends power to the rear wheels. Newer models can reach 198 miles (319 kilometers) per hour or more! An **aerodynamics** package can be added. It offers more control at high speeds.

🔧 ENGINE SPECS

GT R PRO

TWIN-TURBO V8 ENGINE

TOP SPEED — can reach 198 miles (319 kilometers) per hour

0-60 TIME — 3.5 seconds

HORSEPOWER — 577 hp

The GT comes in two different body styles. The coupe has two or four doors and a hard roof.

GT 63 S FOUR-DOOR COUPE

SIZE CHART

GT BLACK SERIES

WIDTH 81.7 inches (207.5 centimeters)

The **roadster** has two doors and a removable roof. Drivers can hear the engine roar!

GT C ROADSTER

HEIGHT 50.4 inches (128 centimeters)

LENGTH 181.3 inches (460.5 centimeters)

CARBON FIBER

GT BLACK SERIES

Most AMG GT models are made with aluminum. Some are made with **carbon fiber**. Both are lightweight. This helps the cars go fast!

All models feature a large Mercedes **badge** on the front **grille**.

STAR POWER

The Mercedes badge is a three-pointed star. It represents land, sea, and air.

BADGE

Over the years, GT owners could choose from many different **trims**.

MADE BY HAND

All AMG GT engines are handmade in Germany. Only one master builder works on each engine.

The GT3 was built to race. The GT R has a rear **wing**. The Black Series has extra power!

THE GT'S FUTURE ≫

AMG stopped producing the GT in 2021. But the company plans to release a new GT model in 2025.

Mercedes-Benz has released exciting **concept cars**. One moves sideways! Another looks like a spaceship. The company's future is bright!

VISION AMG CONCEPT CAR

GLOSSARY

aerodynamics—related to parts that are able to move through air easily

badge—a sign to show that a person or thing belongs to a certain group

carbon fiber—a strong, lightweight material used to strengthen things

concept cars—cars built to show a new design

coupe—a smaller car that has a hard roof and usually has two doors

grille—a set of bars that covers an opening on the front of a car; the grille allows air to enter and exit.

luxury—having a high level of comfort

models—specific kinds of cars

roadster—a two-seated car with an open top

trims—models of a car with specific sets of features and equipment

V8 engine—an engine with 8 cylinders arranged in the shape of a "V"

wing—a part on a car's body that helps it smoothly travel through the air

TO LEARN MORE

AT THE LIBRARY

Murray, Julie. *Mercedes AMG GT*. Minneapolis, Minn.: Abdo Zoom, 2020.

Peterson, Megan Cooley. *Mercedes AMG GT R*. Mankato, Minn.: Black Rabbit Books, 2021.

Walker, Kevin. *Mercedes AMG G-65*. Vero Beach, Fla.: Rourke Educational Media, 2019.

ON THE WEB

FACTSURFER

Factsurfer.com gives you a safe, fun way to find more information.

1. Go to www.factsurfer.com.

2. Enter "Mercedes-AMG GT" into the search box and click 🔍.

3. Select your book cover to see a list of related content.

INDEX

aerodynamics, 12
aluminum, 16
badge, 17
basics, 9
Benz, Karl, 6
body styles, 14, 15
carbon fiber, 16
company, 6, 7, 8, 17, 20
concept cars, 20, 21
coupe, 4, 14
doors, 14, 15
engine specs, 12
engines, 6, 12, 15, 18
future, 20
Germany, 7, 18
grille, 17
GT Black Series, 14–15, 16, 19
GT R, 19
GT R Pro, 12, 13
GT3, 19
history, 6, 7, 10, 18, 20
luxury, 8
models, 8, 12, 16, 17, 20
name, 10
racing, 11, 19
range, 11
roadster, 15
roof, 14, 15
safety car, 11
size, 14–15
speed, 11, 12, 16
trims, 18, 19
wheels, 12
wing, 19

The images in this book are reproduced through the courtesy of: Mercedes-AMG, front cover, pp. 3, 4, 5, 6, 8, 9 (isolated, engine, grille, hood), 10, 12, 13, 14 (main and width), 15 (main and length), 16 (main and carbon fiber), 17, 18, 19, 20, 21; NA, p. 6 (Karl Benz); Emre Zengin/ Alamy, p. 7; Independent Photo Agency Srl/ Alamy, p. 11; Michele Morrone, p. 19 (GT3).